"Let me recite what history teaches. History teaches."
Gertrude Stein

of those saints we know the listing follows

saint orm married saint rain
gave birth to saint iff and saint ave

this is the oldest family

saint iff married saint rive
gave birth to saint reat
who married saint agnes
gave birth to saint rand

saint ave married saint raits
gave birth to saint ranglehold
who did not marry

of the other families
these we mention

saint ill married saint ove
gave birth to saint and & saint rike

saint and did not marry

saint rike married saint ain
gave birth to their son
the nameless one

saint aggers wife is now forgotten
gave birth to saint ump & saint rap
gave birth to noone
dying in the fire reat had set

is nothing but a history
brief at best
an end of one thing
beginning of another
premonition of a future time or line we will be writing

one thing makes sense
one thing only
to live with people
day by day
          that struggle
to carry you forward
                    it is the only way

a future music moves now to be written
w g r & t
its form is not apparent
it will be seen

k l m n
b r v
a hymn for saint iff
a song for his only son
the lonely one who died less lonely
& for his son
who never knew him
a song to
carry him thru to
the end

the martyrology

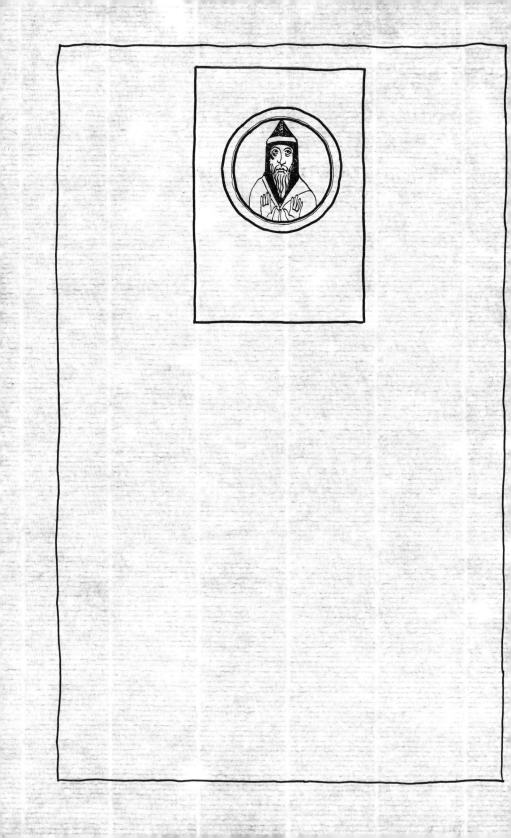

from *The Chronicle of Knarn*

i've looked across the stars to find your eyes

they aren't there

where do you hide when the sun goes nova?

i think it's over

somewhere a poem dies

inside i hide my fears   like bits of broken china
mother brought from earth
                               milleniums ago

i don't know where the rim ends
                                        to look over
into the great rift

                        i only know i drift without you
into a blue that is not there

tangled in the memory of your hair

the city gleams in afternoon suns.   the aluminum walls
of the stellar bank catch
                            the strange distorted faces of
the inter-galactic crowds.

                            i'm holding my hat in my hand
standing awkwardly at the entrance to their shrine
wishing i were near you.
                            were they like us? i don't know.
how did they die & how did the legend grow?

(a long time ago i thot i knew how this poem would go, how the
figures of the saints would emerge. now it's covered over by
my urge to write you what lines i can. the sun is dying. i've
heard them say it will go nova before the year's end. i wanted
to send you this letter (this poem) but now it's too late to
say anything, too early to have anything to send.)

i wish i could scream your name & you could hear me
out there somewhere where our lives are

we have moved beyond belief
into a moon that is no longer there

i used to love you (i think)
used to believe in the things i do
now all is useless repetition
my arms ache from not holding you

the winds blow unfeelingly across your face
& the space between us
is as long as my arm is not

the language i write is no longer spoken

my hands turn the words
clumsily

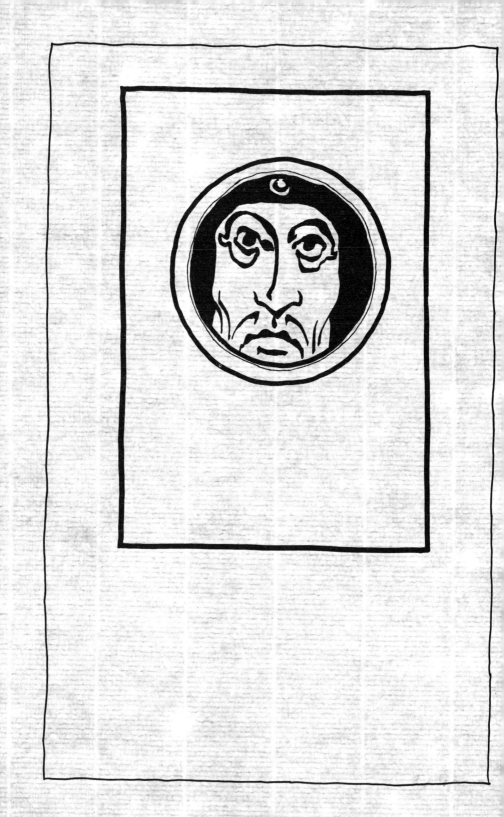

the martyrology

books 1 & 2

bp nichol

The Coach House Press   Toronto

*To the man who lives without saints all
this must appear like flies on the surface
of reality. And are we necessary? we who
have achieved immortality in name only?*

from THE WRITINGS OF SAINT AND

for lea
without whose act of friendship
quite literally none of this would have been written

& for palongawhoya
"he made the whole world an instrument of sound"

BOOK 1

the breath lies

on mornings like this
you gotta be careful
which way you piss

the martyrology
of saint and

As to what auguries attended his birth
nothing is said. Perhaps it was simply
that nothing of importance happened.

so many bad beginnings

you promise yourself
you won't start there
again

december 67

the undated poem is
found and
              forgotten

                         passes

like gas &

hills

bank of clouds

no returns

goodbye
         to this world

gold frame the windows

i've looked out your eyes years now saint and

how
i tell you
no

    things
cannot
        measure thee

                motion

oceans
as in
a western mode of thot
enshrine the deeper blues
moving into
the edge of
blackness
the mind's passage thru
a weight of
        feeling

is eternal your eyes?

so many times "now" occurs

a charm
fingering the present real

the feel of colour in
the fingers' tips
your hands
questions words cannot
understand

joy casts a tent in your midst

hucksters
strip your trees &
leave

centre poles fall

in the ring
saint and
trips in a circle
                on his head

face red

eyes blue

        elephants
drag your words
over impossible hills
into   the valleys   beyond

the mouth
takes up the feeling &
confuses

the fused words move out

where the ears were
a numbness grows

flowers

sweet smells
dumb the lips

saint and
            enshrined in organdy
flows out the chimney

no smoke blows

it is a landscape without hearing

a sea of cries

the lies are simply the listening
without replies

the carnival ride a tree with false branches

lady lady have you met saint and?
he knew death
              when death
                      was just
a man

now one half crawls with maggots
the other wears a grin

slim lady   lady of light   lady who is not

i've lost my head (better off dead)   rides
are still two
for a quarter

make the setting here

                          an ocean
moved in
      becomes a lake

mountains flatten & the hills contract

one gazes out the panes are not the same

the black letters dispatched over a field of white

saint and does not amaze
but is a statue
a corner lost

the fading light conceals his hands

they are as still as hills
if hills are still this far inland

tents cast on the sand

children run toward the sea
clutching their nickels & dimes

                          it is   a freak show
of improbable changes

                the bearded ladies & men
                parade themselves in purple bathingsuits
                offering smiles to the crowds below

in the back room the midget deals another hand
cursing the upcoming spectacle

saint and moves innocuously thru the scene
nodding his head at the awestruck faces

it is not an easy thing to do

the terror in his heart can't be shown

only his blue eyes let it thru

in the dressingroom he removes his make-up

the huge smile & blue hair evaporate

the red paint on his face is streaked & bare

he rests his head in his hands & doesn't care

                                        the sea
moves in upon the tents   then stops

                              despair
                                    is not   an ocean

it is a sea you walk upon till your feet are sore

saint and has lost all hope
& cannot walk or swim there
                        anymore

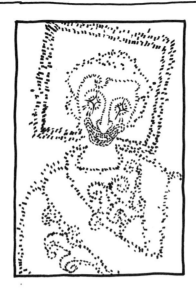

you say goodbye or you say hello.   you say both
not knowing the difference.

saint and moves with the circus from town to town
where the tents were
                    the grass is brown   & the child
has only the memories
to return to

              it becomes maudlin.   death is simply
a way of giving up.

to saint and   every gesture of his hand
is another nail   that has failed
to hold

& the cold wind from the sea
                              is a mockery

or a joke
that should not be told

SAINT REAT

SAINT RANGLEHOLD

SAINT AND

the hierarchy's a difficult place to stand

the names do not smell sweet

                         wearers tire

old saints take to mountains
to dwell in caves on
berries & raw meat

to each speech is a tiresome thing

the gasbellied saints in town
frown & touch their noses in scorn

the morning prayers of the faithful meet deaf ears

in the hills   His will is done
                     some years

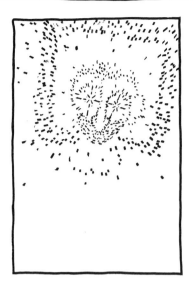

close the door

i didn't open my mouth

                 (saint and measures the levels of the moon

his spoon is full)

        all questions become rhetorical if the pose holds

        I TOLD HIM DIFFERENT

        how can you
        write the news if you
won't listen

my hand
a cup

drink it up & down

nothing holds that's simply stolen

if there is a heaven there is not

lady lady hold me tight
night's so hard to be lonely in

nothing shady

                king fool
fool me a lady

triteness
            saint and   is living
without understanding

nothing

            falls thru the many levels of
            this room

the circus finally grows old & jaded
the faded tents & signs torn & useless

saint and too must age

blue hair thin & falling

birds call over the sea

moving towards the hills
the major notes are lost in minor movements
fading away in trees
& the man knows only the leaves
or the ghost
            of saint and's mourning

it is another world   vaguely seen

                                    the bear
(caged)   cannot cross

                          you stand on this side & look up   way up
into the blue air

it is the colour of saint and's hair

the circus disappears down the road
(elephants straining)

& the hills?

the hills turn red

                    if you ever cross over

scenes from the
lives of the saints

*Saint Reat is encountered more often than any other
saint. His function seems ambiguous, but it would
appear he was a sort of latter-day muse, a saint of
speech & song, tho who he was in real-life remains
unknown.*

saint reat
these halls are slippery

the cool cold of the marble staircase takes the breath away

walking

hand within hand

world without end

                              crossing over
into   a different tongue

du monde de la tigre

eyes yellow as teeth

it's so far from one end to the other
sound repeating itself beyond perfect zero

thin air takes the shadows up

a screaming only you can hear

reach infinitely
no sky towards which
columns the saints pass between

                              saint reat

                              saint and

saint ranglehold
oblivious in his bathtub
sails plastic boats & sinks them

cries of the sailors caught in the heaving line the tongue can't speak

beseeching

saints without name

pain of reaching
beyond touching

hands

real pleasure
            saint reat
the poem can't provide

so many times the flesh aches with loneliness

& this marble this phony architecture you hide behind
well

        saint reat i want to talk to you

        you won't come back at me out of the poem

        if i say "hunger"
will they call it a figure of speech

it's such a long night to lie awake in

& the flesh does ache

& the night is lonely to belong in

dedicate the poem to a whim

                        His mercy

He was always telling me "stand on your own two feet"
when i walked on all fours

                        saint reat
you've taken up with some chick called agnes
& won't listen anymore

                        & saint ranglehold

hell he never listened anyway!

how many ships were lost in his fucking storms?

the point is   independence   in the greater sense

obscure?

saint reat only saint and understands the honesty of chance
& he's broke
                        or starving

this is a real world you saints could never exist in

born in an imperfect reading of the stars   you clashed
farther back than i care to remember

                                    & this?

this is dismembering the heart's history

Superimpose the sea against his whole life.
Only then does the randomness & cruelty of
Saint Ranglehold become apparent. Much of
his life was spent studying under Saint Orm
& were there such a thing as "the good" or
"the bad" saints where would we place him?
We know nothing of him so how can we judge
him?

a ship in perilous storm
the lover doth compare his state to

often he loses
                    (sinking out of view)

dedications change as frequently as the moon

                                        emma peel

riding the white waves
patterns seem strangely familiar

ruler of the ships & sea
saint ranglehold guides lovers with a flacid hand

snickers knowingly
as they flounder on dry land

few choices

travelling nowhere consistently

saint ranglehold
you've got me by the balls & won't let go

followed immediately
by another   pitch variation

he blew harmonica in the all saints band

things got out of hand

put those poems in a drawer

                              close it

vast

sweet emma peel is gone.   who understands?
maybe dick tracy or sam.

                                were there a heaven
who would you place there heavenly angels?

                                                the bells

                                                the bells

dear funny paper i write upon

  a star

            (venus long hair
                              half moon
          soft belly
                        sighing
the car cries

emma peel

random brain stranded in the station

sam & dick & emma peel
oh how the real world gets lost in you

the loose ends shrivel
                        & are gone

faces denote the places growing song

The romance between Saint Reat & Saint Agnes
is one of the most delightful interludes in
the otherwise sombre story of the saints. It
has caused much speculation & given us our
only real glimpse into their
questionable humanity.

it is the soft green growing things

a world apart
pressing
            out of the earth
into the heart

words that bridge the distances between our separate ears

soft growing greenness in our mouths

the dying fears

saint agnes
you were the best thing to happen to a guy

you taught me how to cry

green to blue

away

how could you? saint reat's been
such a sad guy. maybe you'll bring joy into his life.

maybe the maybes can come to be!

suddenly it makes sense. is it the poem makes us dense?
or simply writing, the act of ordering
the other mind
                blinding us
to the greater vision

                what's a
poem like you doing in a
poem like this?

may you be laid to rest in Shanghalla
someday

ranglehold
                when will you come
home from the sea?

                        & you saint and from the hills?

i'm tired of fingering these old poems
stringing them into beads

saint reat & saint agnes
may you go down together from this nothingness

Nura Nal help me!
when will i see where emma peel has gone?

dick tracy's chasing
some murderer on the moon   & you're strung out in Naltor
a long way from home

                        all these myths confuse me

too many saints & heros

Shanghalla   take them away

may their heads be wrapped in threads

green

        blue

                grey

the sorrows of
saint orm

my lady my lady

this is the day i want to cry for you
but my eyes are dry

somewhere i'm happy

not like the sky
outside this window
gone grey

———————————

this is the line between reality
when i hold your body
enter the only way i am

saint orm
keep her from harm

this ship journey safely

quick as it can

saint orm you were a stranger
came to me out of the dangerous alleys &
the streets

        lived in
that dirty room on
comox avenue

               me &
my friends
               playing what lives we had to
the end

        i want to tell you a story
in the old way
            i can't

haven't the words or
the hands to reach you

& this circus   this noise in
my brain
        makes it hard to explain
my sorrow

you were THE DARK WALKER
stood by my side as a kid

i barely remember

except the heaven i dreamt of
was a land of clouds
you moved at your whim

knowing i walked
the bottom of a sea

that heaven was up there
on that world in the sky

that this was death

that i would go there
when i came to life

how do you tell a story?

saint orm you were the one

you saw the sun rise
knew the positions of the stars

how far we had to go
before the ultimate destruction

as it was prophesied in REVELATIONS
nations would turn away from god & be destroyed

told me the difference between now & then
when i could no longer tell the beasts from men

saint orm
grant me peace

days i grow sick of seeing

bring my lady
back from that sea she's crossed
tossed in a grey world of
her own

there is no beauty in madness

no sinlessness
in tossing the first stone

make her sea calm

bring her safe to
my arms

moon lover   dog star
far home   wind dream
7th sister   great river
beast that screams

my lady's a gentle thing
sings me
           when she can

saint orm
you know i wouldn't do her harm
but it seems i get lazy in
the little things

dark skies &
the ocean's stormy

blows up fast
out of the passed over world

that time on comox
leaned out the window on the harbour
twelve blocks away

                        barb & dave
over the street
                        we'd meet in the later hours
getting under way

brings us here

all ties broken by
the hands of fear

you told me not to mention it & dave did
passed thru toronto after five years
both of us near to speaking
told each other how it had been

such a painful thing
being part of history
friends gone
separate ways

saint orm
you were the grey we passed thru
                                    guarded that sea

you were that pilot i took on board
slept on the steps of dezso huba's place
the night dave & barb weren't home
coming down with the flu

didn't know what to do

lost in the absence of being where everyone assumed me not to be
i gave up the ship & sank into misery

half world of seeing
left me blank

                    smiling

lying as i knew would fit
their worries

                    concerns at being
part of the similarity

saint orm
i throw up these poems
out of the moment of the soul's searching

part of the process of gaining focus

never could

lost that dimension a long time

the ryme of
                breathing

the room a fire exit
                    broken glass

lay in the half window

watched the clouds climb
out of your head &
lost you

seaparated by all that blue nothing
crept out of my hand

———————————————

that was the past

always i shall
return again to you

                    my lady

no movement in the sky
from the corner where the four winds lie

& the colour of her eyes too

did i tell you how my lady moves?

holds me to her   tight
she can

          love to feel her
          moving with me

into that sweet togetherness
presses us thru

so much lost

notes in my journals
don't hold true

nothing remembers

except we write in terms of passed moments
instances of unperceived truth
ruthless working of the mind's ignorance
against us

        dave & barb had no chance
no knowing things behind the things they did do

saint orm i need the rage to lead   drive my hand

tenderness
        carry it to the end

nights that run together on the bed

you fill yourself with someone else's loneliness

i've had enough of my own

only thing i wanted to do
somehow bring them with me into something better

always thot would happen
we'd remain as friends
ended those months on comox

boxed with faded photos
somewhere in the corners of these rooms

pass & smile vaguely

coincidences time extends

opened & told them

saint orm these are far shores you carry me to
cold winds to set upon these sails

barb & dave married separate people

i never did settle down

funny the way
the thots break

it is a voice   a presence close to sleep
speaks from that too familiar world

i will return my lady
but these worlds burn

i cannot stop the flow

single vibratory wave that goes   back
into all history

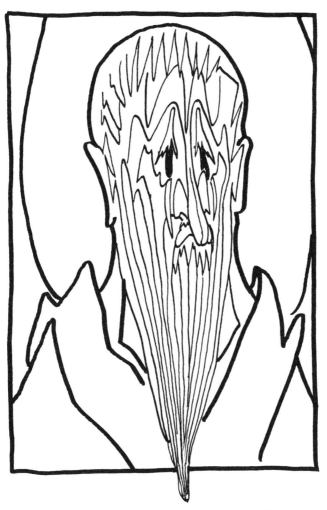

saint reat and the four winds of the world

Once upon a time, so the story goes, Saint Reat
lost his voice but was given it back on the con-
dition that he go on a quest for the origins of
all breath.

from THE FOLK TALES OF THE SAINTS

stirred the leaves are
come to this land

sounds we walked in
before the last death visited the world

(weary walking to you)

where the winds blew
out of the corners of
                           the mind

i do know you

how you dwelt in that place filled with questions
the rest (written in a book) destroyed my childhood
began this drifting focusless twist of speech i
you reach towards saint reat

bruised fruit & dry branches

discoloration of
the apple's skin

                    bite into your arm
stop the pain
               again & again

under the moon

lie on the hill

feel the wind blow
from that country where no man goes that lives

tumble tongue   fish face
sayer of dreams

comer in nightmares
screaming & babbling

slime nose & green lip

dribbler of phrases
symbols & spewing

blood cougher   swamp dweller   "loon"

moments the eyes ache
not from seeing

                    least of what is shall be
most hopefully free wind
for him   trapped lover earth caresses
folding dark skin

wind home
how shall i reach you with all speech gone?

stars

the moving pattern of
the eye's lid

a visitation

how do you act?

raised up his finger or
his arm

told you what you must do &
no harm could touch you

gave you your life your tongue
to seek the wind that day when you were younger

given a sign in
the midst of your life

came to that road you did not know
where saint agnes stood
                         proud &
alone

& when you feli in love you died

a part of you cried you were lonely
& gave up the only life you'd known

can you say it is true you died?
like the image i read in a poem
years ago   the metaphor   symbolic thrust of
a real penis   entering all that flesh &
he "died"   said that he "died"
to rise again   phoenix fucker
old bird getting into her
only way he knew
when after all it was his prick
should've been a a part of him
flew away   heart pounding
head of the dread thing swollen with blood
turned into   a miracle   white flood of love
slipping into her & all the grass
blew around him   last thing before he passed
into   that other world

this is a strange country
desert flows around us death &
breath makes us wary

the spires & the high walled
mute people fill the streets

is it because the wind blows
whispers lost in shouting?

how did you get here when the secret's knowing

wet fingers

the whole face
rippled by
the air

i speak lip tongue
no throat

lost touch with
the whole thing

never learned to dance to
my voice

sing

praises

rejoice

the man who lived in that town   a tailor by trade
told you where the truth lay

some people lie no matter how they speak
no matter tongues move their heads

look in eyes

learn the meaning behind the meaning said

stood on the wall
saw the great snake coiled in the distance
the reason the silence insisted

gave you a sword
the word to make him sleep
the one to wake him

how you could take him captive
                              tame him
if you chose

led you there

shifting

stand in the wind
sand whip the eyes

what was it rose out of the brown
froze the ground under you

your past or present moment

unseen motion of the trembling land

took him within the spine's motion
pulsating rush of skin

over the sand the boulders to the sea

over the water where the edges fall from the mind

ten days

cloudy roads

future holds
ways you saw of going

it was the end of that phase of being

you dreamt

woke without knowing what the dream meant

in this country it was all caves

each road led into shadows
soft formless hands
                    called your name &
you answered

a thing without eyes or lips

saint reat this is all a dream
you could've seen if you'd stopped to think

what threatens now
comes from the worlds at the edge of vision

half perceived auras round the rims of life

took saint agnes for a wife
when still a kid
then started this stupid quest

saint orm kept saint ranglehold in line
a long time
                long enough to teach him a few tricks
if no manners

& saint and   well
he wandered with some plan
even if he did get side-tracked into the circus

but you!

                god grant you rest

cloud-hidden come up out of the west & show you
the way home

these other saints
ump & rap

it seems silly

when death comes
the dumbest things flash by your eyes

they were brothers
mothered by the town fool
before the great war nearly destroyed the planet

hated the lives fate granted

set out to kill you
that night as a kid
you blew the lid off their plan to rob the halls

died in the fire
you never meant to set

were canonized

because they had lived exemplary lives of self-denial
before that final moment of weakness

he was a blindman met on the road

a saint named aggers

told you sins were
denials of our sounds

of a town in the. desert where the silence was

how peace lay in your sounds home
beyond the ocean where the four winds roam

———————————————————————

(she looked in your eyes & knew your story
how their deaths meant you could not rest
tho you tried

                    took you in her arms

you wanted to stay there but left
months before the child was born)

i get lost

poem-maker   cloud-hidden
you were one & the same

isn't it plain why saint and called you fool?

this is a cruel world you rule
a rough road

saint reat's load's too heavy for his years

raises his fears too high

                              drove him out of his mind
into that other

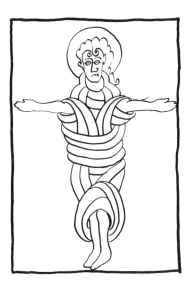

the trick was seeing there was nothing there
& the sense hit you of the fight won

against the darkness hurled from your brain you stood

still

————

this is a love poem

wrote it on the long road   singing

nearly home

stood in the place the north wind blew

was it a face
                or simply a presence
spoke
        lifted the skin you wore
& changed you

you were never the same

those cells were prisons

unyielding stone

took & broke them

freed form

remember the time as a child
an old man passed you on the road

a saint your father said

raced out to ask him his name
what saints did

told you his name was raits
he'd been a seeker since his youth

so you asked him what he'd found in all that time

showed you the line from
his wrist to his thumb

walked on

you grew up frightened

always that distance between
no way to bridge
the greyness of the rim worlds

curled before the fire
imagined a higher order of things

never knew this life
because you occupied another

the day the two kids died
how did you feel when they were canonized?

envy?   sorrow?

how will you feel tomorrow when you're dead?
will it do your heart good
knowing you're a saint?

it's only names they give you
titles for books

the way your mother bore you
you must return
                    from dust to dust
thru worlds of burning energy

& the south & the west & the eastern winds
wrapped your limbs in motion

walked you cross the ocean to a western shore

bore you up
into the silent town

turned the desert green

wrapped it round

you returned the long road
found her there

the child was ten

how long had you wandered
lost from men
wrapped in that other place

she touched your face with her eyes
her hands

lay down beside you as the song ends

saint reat this is all nothing

do you understand?

there are no myths we have not created
ripped whole from our lived long days

no legends that could not be lies

you were simply a man
suffered the pain of silence in your head

let your sounds lead you out of that dead time

were made a saint
for lack of any other way of praising you

1967 - 69

BOOK 2

speech

eech to
each

book of common prayer

for Bill Bissett

"a funny name for claimd similur creaturs
    one a porpoise   th othur a dolphin"

saint of no-names
saint of kisses

your lips are on me
sharp-tooth & giggle-eye

final voices in the living room
sick in bed with grief
walked out the door that last time & told you

bled my mouth dry of words

later:

try to write the poem i breathe in

noise

what level of

did you moving back there thru her
yes & handed him the change

all these noises &
screaming

stiff-shouldered in the chair
where's the muse will save me

USELESS SAINTS
YOUR FUCKING LIES &

jesus sweet eyes
skin of blessing
did i catch it in a cup
for saving?

all things fall

all things are one in the end

all that is all encompassed in that word

ah sweet saints of sameness
you are that saint

his all

friandise

dolci

just as such things begin
so there are others end

useless motion to the bathroom
shit my life away

hey i remember
no i don't

you were never much good you saints

i watch the sun set thru my window
dreaming i am somewhere else

WHERE ARE YOU?
when every place i look are lies

please

such fits of longing

fascination with the worst & best

come home to heaven
thru a gate of clouds
saw saint ory
in a silken shroud

you be grinnin
but i be free
ain't no saint
make a fool of me

no more

no other story

goodbye in your glory
in your brooding stillness

i was always too successful at disguises
knew which mask to wear & where

pulled on my prose & clothes each morning
stepped out of the bed onto the bare floor

open the door look for the morning paper
it's not there

& since i believe in god i confess it now for all time
the saints & angels &

pull on my socks & poetry
down to the kitchen & work

pass the time away

wait between breaths for the muse to strike
give me reason to breathe & pray for night to come

back to bed

dream

who are you i have addressed by names these years
the mocking image of the truthful man
writing when he can & can't tho
such dreams of sainthood as he did dream dead
writing now for what's to be & over

let us forget them

let us put them behind us forever

let us join hands & be free

goodbye

goodbye to you saints

goodbye to you saints of pain & wisdom

holy prayer mother

holy prayer father

praise be to this to praise
in your longing
infinite

if we allow ourselves indulgences
let them be those of clarity & truth

if we wallow in self-pity
may we be cursed forever

useless this morning
this evening the snow comes

plane sound thru the glass passes thru me

sit at my desk
studying my hands

these poems

it all ends

i said that before

someone opened his mouth & said that
so long ago i don't care

if it is repeated
is it left behind?

sweet truth of oneness
duality that does not see

sweet sweet vision

sweet clarity

everything i say
i have said before
once when i thot each phrase new
& now see the mockery of speech

artifice

holding over
the tight phrases & cursed verse

SCREAMING

soft saintly night
oh god good night
soft saint soft light

cloud together
the bed these edges of
hold me

god it would be good if you'd hold me

you know it gets lonely
at the edge of hell
look out my window onto the room
i do miss you yes i do
who would've i mean
seeing you there in your long robe &
i should've said golden hair but it's not true

didn't i see you
when last week oh
no you know i think it was that time before at least i
please

it would be good
it would be
to be beholding

there is nothing but is dreams
my whole thot slurred together finally
truth is living thru those intervals between the sighs

& i'm holding you aggie
ah sweet agnes
holding you to me
being mister reat

these puns are obvious & seal the mind
blinding the eye
which is the imprecision of the word

i knew when i headed home tonight
the whole poem graphed in my mind
i'll never make it

some things are stronger than words

if i could throw down this pen i never use
then i could live my life   free of naming

there is nothing which is allegory

when you have lived these voices & these hands
you end up always in the expliations

rooms

holding the twisted bedsheets
or the dirty ashtrays

all the sentimental crap

afterthings

what happened

simply that final thing

no gift for narrative i said
no life to be
being finally the whole process
as it is & has been
mostly flow

watch the words go
as the days do

as the as's grow

mirrors into mirrors
into mirror
into or

i wanted to end it

step into my room happy
still this nameless ache upon the chest

i wanted to reach you one more time

i'm sorry
not for the life i've led
i've led this life i've
no i'm simply sorried
held in this room i'm sitting writing to you

prayers

as if you were there & heard me

clouds

this time the sky screams   BLUE
thru a break in the clouds   high above me
so high i cannot fly there with the mind
the saints live   & they called it cloud town
when they fell to earth as strangers
wide-eyed at all this tumbling green land
spun thru space towards their falling bodies &   caught them
SKY BLUE   the colour of saint and's eyes
taking in this surprising place he'd come to

if there is a land which is the mind
it is as brown as earth & cool there

somewhere i know there are streams that flow clearly
carry the memories to me

peace
as in a postcard of that place

so brightly real
you can't believe that it exists

surely when they fell
it was into grace

left the white streets of that higher town
to tumble down the long blue highway to the trees'
tops   saint re at &
saint and   travelling thru those lands of colour
they'd followed the rainbow down to find
the land at the end of the rainbow
the ancient saints had taught about
this day   they'd set their feet upon the earth
as if it were the lost home
the lost planet of their birth

One night saint and fell asleep & had a dream. In the dream his great great grandfather spoke to him. 'How shall I find cloud home again?' asked saint and. 'You will never return in this time,' said his great great grandfather, 'but must wander that earth you've come to until you meet this woman' & he showed saint and an image of her face & saint and rose & never returned to that place again.

'How Saint And Heard About Cloud Woman' THE FOLK
TALES OF THE SAINTS

no other story

fit to tell

yeah & when you looked in there
into those clouds they called her eyes
was it a surprise to see your death mirrored

the trees are green but .
the skies are stormy

for me   for me

if i could stretch out once in a field
gaze up there thru that blue blue blue
& fall back to you

                    where you came from then when
the earth was younger   & the roads the roads were
so brown & yellow under the sun you fell thru
did you i mean fall there like that into her arms

god they are so cloud hidden
those skies you come from
met her in the grey space between the worlds
where the clouds curl round you
& the mind is not yet home

six o'clock

find your way back again
thru the tall grass & broken fields
pass thru the stream you should be following
on

as if there were no adequate words to fit the mind's
conceptions   a blurring glass
washed over   & your hand passed thru her
there was nothing there to hold
went thru her   into that cloudy hole you'd called the sea
when your life was higher

                                        sweet sanity
these are tricks the mind plays
fire storms within the brain

sweet sweet madness
nothing is the same again
having crossed that misery

christ i wanted to be there
walk the white world with you
look over the field today
see the separate grey point of land
jutting above me

                         each time it is again
i enter the softer world of women
seeing your face saint and
i remember the tales they tell
how you fell from the cloud world to the earth
from the earth into her eyes
who was not a woman but simply the disguises trouble wears
braiding up its hair
so you would touch her

how i would wish you happiness
who has had so little all these years
only such tears you could not shed
and yet
was there pleasure there
some way of freeing you from being in your body
giving up your birthright each night
to slip inside her in your joyful suffering

if that's true
you know they never should have sainted you

you were such a stupid little fucker
nailed your hands upon the cross you bore
up & down the streets
tearing your clothes
in joy   in grief

now the wind blows the clouds away
i can see clear into heaven
a deeper darker blue by night
those towns you walked the streets of
listening to your elders' tales

even in the markets they told of a time
some younger saint would follow the rainbow down

ah but look at this

you pissed it away in suffering
hooked up with a chick the village fool could see thru
& avoided

that lady almost destroyed the muse
& you let her use you
willingly for your own destruction

these are the times i could curse your name
were it not so pointless blaming you

in that brownness which is the mind
green things flourish

it is a place to breathe in deeply
look up & gaze into the endlessness of space

a light blue place cloud people tend to
watch over you as you pass
into the tall tall tall
& sweetly

only the should've been

she was no cloud lady
only cloudy

only as a tree is only
become a ship & lost at sea

drowning bodies slipping off its body

silenced dreams

the country you spoke of
having travelled over the hills for days
ends where the sky ends merging with the sea
& you stepped up   into the air
to touch the clouds

                        your lack of vision
ties you to the earth

                        all these women
these cloudy cloudy women

there was no one there

you walked the streets of cloud-town found them bare
the empty houses & forgotten treasures
as tho some terror had stopped there
drove them fleeing into eternity

When saint reat took the trail from cloud-town to earth he was
still a child &, in the first town he came to, found a family that
adopted him. it was less than a year before the details of his
life in cloud-town became so vague they were virtually forgotten.

from "The Great Migration" THE FOLK TALES OF THE SAINTS

faces cloud in on me

lost as i am mostly dreaming
streets fill with memory brush against me

library daze
the dust & centuries pile up within the mind's
gestures

as if she were part of history
history being in me is my story
my vision of the world's end &
beginning   as you did saint reat
arriving here   over
the lost chords struck within the brain
look out from a child's face
the world discovered
rediscovered
this century this day

pile up the movement the fingers
inside the body's thinking
water flow the sucking sound &
and and and and
end

      this last chance to start now
new the moment faces you

reach for the knife
butter your bread

live thru this moment
this momentum carries you

this

& this &

this

how shall i call you father who have left me here
lonely on this bright blue world
i am falling into hell & never know it

father
you have forgotten your sons
saint reat & saint and
too young to know the difference

the skies mass with death
the stink of horror
pollutes the air

i did not know terror
till i awoke
concious you had left me here

grew up twice
once in the world we came to call heaven
once on earth

could've come from anywhere
planets exploding at your birth
what signs what miraculous inventions

you wandered into town &
they took you in

bright sun

clear windy day

like any other

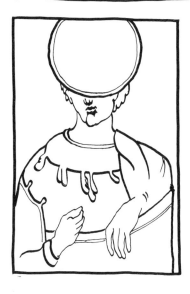

living as you did in winter worlds
always on the far side of the ellipse
who can remember the day
least of all myself who was not there

poor old raits

he'd taken the rainbow but found only pain
as he had in the world that went before
stepped from one door into another
moving always within the frame

did he hear you when you asked the question
or was it just a casual gesture
opening the palm of his hand
damned as you'd always known & his life line showed
moved thru disbelief into sorrow

father i stand where i did before
long ago in that one beginning
now i am only names i number

who can i forgive
having loved my suffering

i wish this poem would end
so i could send my love to you
across the blind weight of history

seeing the ease with which saint reat & saint and made the
transition to earth many other saints chose to follow. among
the first of these was saint orm who, with his pupil saint
ranglehold, made his goodbyes on a rainy troubled day &
descended the dangerous trail from cloud-town to earth.

from 'The Great Migration' THE FOLK TALES OF THE SAINTS

"looking for a town called rain hat"
slid out of the sky onto my shoulders

sit in the mud at the side of the road
watch the clouds open

if it were sunny i could spend the day here

talk to you

oh fuck it's raining

stick my hand into the sea

that's poetry

nothing comes easily

beginning everything with absolutes
the final resolution
                    "to be true"

truly saint orm
i mean you no wrong but

butts against the silence of this room

just a word

just a sign

listening to her clothes drop
each time the moon's up

water from the country
held in the hands

city days

the grey dirt & damp soot
disturbs my prayer
who would speak to you
knowing you're there

saint orm i always pray to you

leaning back upon the ferry deck
followed the gulls thru into the narrower channels

blue sky all around

music from the taperecorder

close my eyes upon the image of her face
unthought of all these years

pray to you to love me
as i do you

redwing blackbirds
that sweet cry

saw him in the bush by the roadside

go from there to here

walk along the road

carry your heart   whole
into the earth

others followed, too numerous to mention. of those who made the
final trek many died tragically. like saint iff, who, arriving
in a desert, died within the sound of water.

from 'The Great Migration' THE FOLK TALES OF THE SAINTS

it is the minute haunts you
final image of
the trapped phrase

smile differently

always tensions building in the poem to pass thru
impossible wall i do
need you now my fingers can't touch you

words slam the page

freeze

if i avoid the image saint iff
if i do write do say to you & yet
please can you maybe understand

what was ever the time i now remember
looked thru the trees into the street not passing
turned backwards into the mind

which is the way
my way of reaching

thus that it is
having tried to fix time
it is myself i am the one destroyed

the words the nothing mostly meaningless
dialogue this conversation ends
abruptly

       who did i love having said i loved you
holding your body in the narrow bed

fear

"now that spring is here
winter anguishes that froze upon the air
reinstate their agony"

o holy ladies ease or end this pain
who would be a happy man
sane again

saint iff
it is the preposition's proposition
another guise

the least is mumbles
jiggles up the tongue across the breast

kiss the rest

every pore of every body charged with memory
loving history between her thighs

forgets does not remember
who began this moment wakens
faceless strange face faces facing

end it here

there is nothing said

over

said

over

said

in the end most of the saints followed the migratory trail from cloud-town to earth. of those who stayed behind little is known except for the curious legend of saint rike & the lady of past nights.

from 'The Great Migration' THE FOLK TALES OF THE SAINTS

this morning there are no clouds anywhere
gaze out my window over the fields
these tastes upon the air tie my tongue to someone no longer here
all speech become a reaching over distances

no cloud-town to return to
only empty sky i cannot remember
do you remember saint rike
remember me

morning gaze in the mirror
who is that there that man
did i own him once his face reach out yes the hands

those ladies we said we loved saint rike
your lady of past nights who returned &
lord god this arm where does it reach to from my body
leave me oh christ what is this soul

oceans to become a sea

remember me

fortunate day

hung by the heel from a tree
the eye sees all around

clear to the ground

swords rise
into the air where
the face should be

wanting to describe the thing accurately
as it did happen it did happen to me
this delicate balance the mind tumbles from

how have i said love so many times
who keeps distances between himself & feeling

winter days disturbing summer
another land the eye is caught in
longer than planned

if i could walk again
those roads as i have walked before
over the fields & down towards the valley
that valley where i wrote those other poems
sit down under the trees i'd speak to you

here there is a peace the mind can breathe in
nothing but the tangles in my tongue
let the sounds sweep in around me
in a heaven with no need of poetry

the lady came to you in the night saint rike
took you away
                    not as the others who had gone before but
far away
            into the sky
some other star
                    where they say those who were left followed

today there is noone to speak to but my reflection
soon gone

smash this mirror

moving on

father i am sorry for this mood
brooding when i should be happy
who has had so much given to him freely

your other sons
where did they go?

today i walk out the door
warm wind upon the face
knowing i am not walking in this place i walk in
no sense of my own worth

lonely going slowly crazy
on this falling earth

"all things loved once spoken for
strung across the past and perished"

saint rike you left no word

gone like the clouds
this first spring day

i am gone like the wind
like the "like"
father

within one millenium the original saints had passed away.

THE FOLK TALES OF THE SAINTS

speak your name across this ocean
what i have seen become in me
parting still too obvious truth

not you saint reat but that other

this is the poem begins & ends here

these nights i lie awake in bed
pray to you whoever you are listen
know that i have hope & live in peace
tho the days are senseless as the weeks

lady i know nothing more

began this poem in sureness
now the truth's obscure behind the body's veil

it is that sense impossible becomes the poetry
shields me from the i within the lie

having loved once & poorly
carry those wounds as disguise

walk out the door this moment
back from the country to the city streets
where am i going

tonight i gaze at the moon
trap my fingers in the window frames

(these streets i walk down having gone before   myself   some
other body   1964 or 5   walk thru a door into the mind   a
woman that i loved returns now constantly   caught in illusions
i cannot control
                           saint reat i know my history leads me
i am nothing else   no longer stumbling over penances it is the
image her image catches)

imagine i walk in a sea

clouds roll over me

i am drowning

who is it in this other room i've found
holds out her hand i cannot take it

dead as i have dreamed that life to be
walk below the white world closing in

for my friends love's life's known least
sought all their days fold in so slowly
hold who they can weeping or with joy

i am i because i fear the we
deeper mystery without solitude

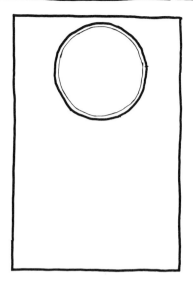

measure friendship by the time it takes to grow
the quality of truth that flows between you
do not destroy each other with your jealousies

fallen asleep in the midst of the poem
wake up to a bright window

all poetry a function of history
breathing now
                    referenceless world
i do take refuge in
surrounded by memory

AUGURIES

lift up your eyes my lady
maybe never again this moment the sun
stood in the window stand & wonder
naked your flesh is my thots run
hold up the moon
                        its perfect circle on the world's rim
that light   one light in all the sky
                                    venus

be in us always
as the times are
a saint's face among the stars & clouds
it changes constantly

saint orm i know you least of all i knew
but now some joy permits allows of me this speaking to you
as it had been those days i did not know your name
lay in fever under what is over
the spell of language on me in confusion
i could not say

these words these words
shriek out the window
wonder who this is returns
history in the form of memory
turning turning
my fingers burn inside you
all that body is & longing

a place i can step into

a place i know of & can step into

these are those other mysteries
not the false veils i chose to hide behind

one month in a room
i dreamt the world ended
thrown into your arms saint orm
nameless then as faceless hands enfolded me
carried away in that ecstasy of dying
pebbles against the pane
knew dave had never made it home
never again opened the door come in
my last night in town won't you
come in i said come in this
place our fingers thru the world to spell us
reminds us now to make it possible
these words across the space you knew
you & your pupil ranglehold chose to travel

"love is carried around in a form
  yu recognize her eyes speak of it"

"a trick / a lovely gesture in the air"

the moments mass there
flicker in the eye
out of sync the words whirl
to be spoken

"seeking the actual story
  changes what is seen"

we were lonely

we had never known home

you stepped out of the hazy
drifted in thru the door my dreams left open
smiling

i never learned a thing

hello you said   i could not answer

hello you said   the words were empty

all that softness i was not permitted to enter
all those worlds i saw but could not feel

imagine myself there
late march of '64
stepping thru the door into barb & dave's place

friends

this song ends as the patterns shift

we hold out hands

turn from the window into your arms my lady
free my head of hazy other worlds of memory
soft insistency of something not understood

it is my own longing
as it was then i could not feel it
felt

      knelt in the window on Comox praying

kneel by your side my lady you become the muse
let the world turn over kiss your breasts
my head returns again my body follows

open your heart

do what is necessary to love

when the moment comes to surrender your feelings
surrender

that was always your trouble saint and
lived on the fringe of tenderness all your days
locked away in anger
never took the hand those people offered
too busy masking you turned them down

self indulgence
this is the greatest sin
you tried to deny
bending over backwards to be used

rise each morning early
give thanks for your birth

who lives in anger
carries the lie quickly to his lips

thus you study nuance
gain mastery of the art of speech
untangling deceit & error

having lived in that world of choice
your voice cracks when feelings rise
confusions &
step sideways to regain your balance
the chance is taken

the part of yourself least recognized
merges with the mirror
your fingers do not know your skin

hold onto things you love
this moment passes as the senses rise
touch ascends with vision
taste smell & sound the image test the real
world without end

arose early   (7:30)

you weren't there

here the sky opens
i can see the town
in ruins now it wasn't then
you lean forward into my present life &
bless me

times change the moon does
earth slips away
the bodies cycle over
currents move as history weighs ahead

gaze at the sky

return from somewhere

live in the present
it is all around you

saint and you stand in windows mourning
cloud-eyes braiding her hair

"I think you will enjoy my babblings
  you made my time easy
  I think of your face it smiles in my head"

pleasure is the skin you move in
flows around & thru you

learn to know yourself

what that means

"oh god we are leaving!"

who listens with his third ear
hearing ever this never i refuse to utter

"got yr telegram in van — a little late — & well, we left
suddenly our little piece of paradise in the hills of
kaministiqua & got back to the coast — stayed long enough
to get some dollars together (tore down the family
garage & slept in the truck) & develop a mild case of the
big city jangles, not to mention monetary fatigue & now
we're up near Kalowna amidst gravel & endless camp fires
looking for jobs fruit picking as only welfare stands
between us & whatever poverty is."

"I hate saying GoodBye but yours was good"

"Goodbye!

LOVE
Suzette"

"love
david"

"Magdalen"

drift then as dreams
my life is lived
moment to moment the changes flow around me
it goes on too long

breaking down the ideas do
hold up the image you have made me closer to with tenderness
someone else's prayer to speak from
dave & denny's party barb came to

i remember now that i remember nothing
driving home late last night
step up to you lord
i have opened my heart for the first time
surely feelings follow

words fall
i cannot pick them up
you bend to kiss me
turn away

dave's face thru all that rain
the pain i could not tell him
it seems so jumbled
what i had thot simple to say
at best but half recalled

bright day

walk up into the clouds you seem so lost saint and
these quests take you thru the sky
follow saint rike you don't know where
step off into a deeper blue
whisper in my ear do tell me
falling with you

home

saint orm died finally
he lives somewhere

where was it you died saint orm
i'm sorry i do not remember

far out at sea
your sails give way
the ocean takes you in

i dream your eyes close slowly
as they must have opened in the beginning

the sky is as this word is
somewhere thru the stars your eyes look back

we need you now
now as we have never needed you before
i need you

i am one am many
the need to be obsesses
simply as i would i would speak to you

speech directed finds one target aim is true

allow what is to be
is not to ceases is
allow to be to do

awoke this moment for the first time
left that confusion behind to love another
she welcomes me in it is hard to bear

you wander pointlessly saint and
struggle from cloud to cloud
you'll never find them

there is a heaven beyond this heaven you did not know of
a heaven beyond that heaven
another time
you shout his name across the clouds
wander the white fields
lonely now saint orm is dead
left those other saints behind
gaze into my face i ask no questions
take my outstretched hand you turn away

i walk the brown roads of earth
face burning in the sun
wishing i could help you find him
that other one, saint rike,
is it true you two were brothers

these days to love seems difficult
all my friends i know too well
it is some hell thru which i pass in search of heaven
trying to learn to bear the pain of joy
it is so hard there is nothing i can teach you

come back please
i have known you too long
would help you now to live within some pleasure

you scream his name against the stars
he does not answer
i answer turn
i answer turn
away away

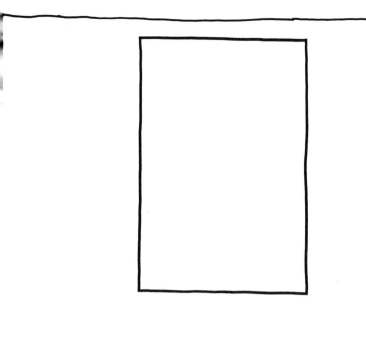

to marry ends the longing for a little
no i do not understand you will

dave drunk & raging
beating on the door to barb's place
he wrote a poem

now there is a voice sings
transcribe the aching
                              i learn by learning

saw barb again
toronto 65
passed thru with wayne
later she married him
how's dave
                    fine

mid-april 64
she & i & henry john
sat in a car at the foot of comox
i was going
image of that journey in my eyes
i loved her

saint rike rides across the sky
dave's poems & mine
letters from the selves we never knew
i asked the saints to listen
stood in the rain on comox dreaming
hidden in my skin i could not see
the dark clouds move over me

she is a ghost who walks among my feelings
fingers me lightly
i am not touched

these talismen
bought so cheaply
worth more than the paper they're printed on

if i could say it to you
you as i said it to before
i could step thru the door into the world this poem opens

her breasts are soft & welcome me in
her belly moves with mine

there is a dream in which the quests intertwine

there are different endings

i should drink less than i do eat less
yes than i do i do do it
living that way & feelings rise
it is all so hard

who takes me as i am
not this self confronts me in the mirror

saint rike he's found you now
tracked you down thru all the blue nothing
we knew didn't exist

twists around me
binds me in

too many poems with the same ending begin

third letter from suzette this month
how i cling to words who have little to say
the words or me that illogical confusion
as love is when words rule the mind

three times repeat the spell is broken
magic your eyes my lips
this probe returns a world is found

was it what you expected saint and?
saint rike turned old & grey
did you travel very far to find him?

record facts
simple at first the observation becomes more complex
the simpler image holds

sometimes the worlds fold forever
into other worlds

how can i offer keys
what rules divides the line is
that way of breathing takes everything inside

in actual fact the thot moves
as the mind does it own perceptions charted
sorry i didn't realize you were there

that moment then saint and
that moment you stumbled thru a cloud into the world saint rike
/discovered

you didn't believe your eyes did you

this is a difficult thing
no longer trusting senses
we dream up ruses
abuses make them seem more real

he was there with his lady
so soft & so pretty
she was strong & she loved him
you started to cry
you started to cry
you started to cry
you started to cry
you started to cry
you started to cry
you started to cry
you started to cry
you started to cry
you started to cry
you started to cry
you started to cry
you started to cry

i occupy a world you move in is that other
as expressions are this redundancy grows

over inform the first law of economy
i gesture magically
you yawn

we move in threes
the short statements linked to
the worlds i live in
hidden personal one & the same

of those things we understand this is the greatest mystery
knowledge deceives us
believing we move in our lostness purposefully
discover new worlds as and did
knowing nothing he came to that place saint rike now lives in

you should've stayed with the circus and
this gets you nowhere
wander forever as you wandered before
your name become a legend
to me at least

the loop crosses over folds into itself
a surface you can travel on forever

the dream ceases

look in the mirror
knowing you have found the beast

what have i constructed
runs a ribbon thru your hair saint and
this end of heaven tied to my door

raise you up into the closet
a window opens into the blue
i dream i see you walking home again
it's not true

you stayed there so long
learned to sing the songs saint rike had learned so well

hell it doesn't matter
only the knowledge you are well & happy
are you well & happy
you aren't are you

sieze the moment
it was said before
i say it again to inform you

tiny song

i sing it all day long

tiny sing

it's a thing i wrote for you

kinda happy

glad i love a lady

but knowing you're unhappy and
makes me kinda blue

found you finally in all this darkness
the world dave & i knew must exist

you step from the mirror
startle me

dave divorced now
living near kalowna
i live on the edge of a great wood

this morning i rose early
dove into the lake
surfaced thru the calm
found the clouds gone

i guard you always in my dreams i waken
you ride a horse by your brother saint rike
thru that far world you might return from

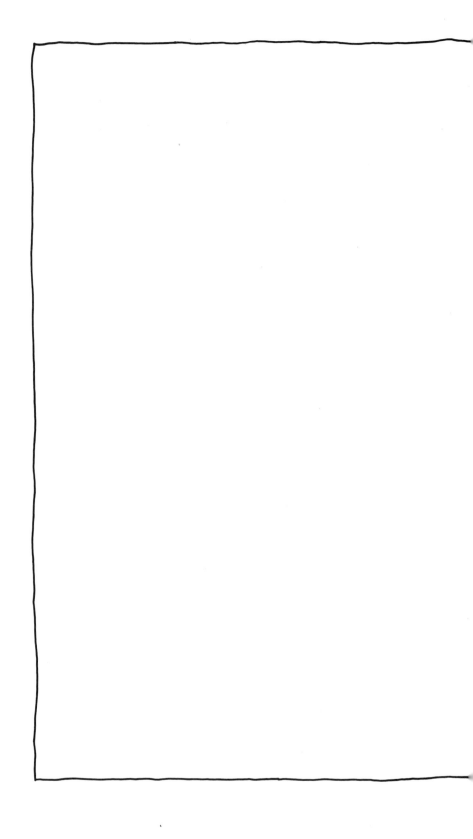

sons & divinations

for friendship's sake my house is set
the blue dragon on my right
the white tiger on my left
the rest is written as my life would be
to be shared

sit by the window on a rainy afternoon to write
poems as acts of friendship
the time is not right

so many things come together
break open the mind each night
tangled together in the morning

as i had noticed it to be
the strange hill rose conical out of the farmer's field
into the middle distance of the earth
patterns are not apparent

now i could make my home there
set roots among the signs our fathers left
one final music to be written
long & beautiful a mourning for the worlds we lost
the fields the saints once walked in was it long ago?
the line to flow together straight & true
around the world & back to you

there is a music in the moment comes together
joyce thot he knew or that insistence stein found
approximation of the one voice vision
repetition condensation theory ways of speaking we can choose

now there is a language speaks apparent
as in mirage or magic thus the choice is made
geomancy the lost art of which noone teaches
apparent thru entendre je ne compris
my world is split

blake saw the chance to be here in canada
serpent power sacred to be wrestled with
real energy my body releases
i can gain the reins of

tho the visionaries are destroyed
or leave willingly as and did
the as's build
one chain apparent thru the life work
i grasp the edge of vision & am frightened

no man holds the dragon but is held by it
learns to direct & shape its will within him
sacred energy to be fed properly
fires which are lit within us daily by the holy act of food

profanation then the chemicals or wilfull choices of impurity
i learn the stranger laws the serpent teaches
energy coil within the mind
sleeping still or buried
as they did in Dilmun bury snakes in baskets under stone
traces of the knowledge now confused in symbols
flux & pull of cosmos
o palongwahoya
your name is many as you are the one
even your brother or your mother spider woman
nothing matters but that He has created
& we sing Him sing His praises
mother brothers of the world

father i speak as i seldom know
"as" is the form is spoken
this lady she is the one the one i love
our words are broken
the language destroyed made whole again
repetition

the rythmic structure awkward or forced is not natural
the tongue bends unwillingly the lips wrap round it
the "a" removed or bitten off

my father was born in the states
came north into canada with his father
who was born in canada & went south into the states with his father
who was born in ireland & came thru the states into canada & back
                                                              /again
into the dakotas my father came out of with his own father
& your father saint rand
you didn't know till you were ten
left you alone with your mother agnes
you grew up hating him
as sons do
            not knowing their fathers intent
hate what they know & long for them

fathers die

their sons grow older
or die young
            too young to have sons of their own
& noone remembers my great uncle john
went west to oregon
                    died of pneumonia
as your father died saint rand
do you remember
went west into the lands he'd dreamed of
to recall those days when he was younger
set out upon the road & found his voice
he went again

you didn't cry

hate stops you up

you are the bitterness you do not say
knowing the day is gone when being his son was all you wanted

these things hurt more than they should

drunk with grief i slap my face
all grace gone in that instant's knowing
i am the son   the sum total of my anger's turning
inwards   coming out in words

clearly the mirror focus blur
fear for your safety

this is harder to write

what flows between confuses you

saint rand you did it too
left earth behind
seeking the land saint and had gone to

as i could not do
rooted in bitter things
sweet taste of blood upon the tongue once the work's begun

what is this feeling of despair
my lips move to speak you

father the night's too long to toss sleepless with such knowledge

pass of death fingers raised
saint rand your face before me in a vision
breaks apart

        alleleujah

        alleleujah

(i stood startled room empty of His presence my own face the open
                                         /door)
"poor john's dead & gone
left me here to sing this song

pretty little gal with your red dress on"

with your dress

with your red dress

on

the window reverses itself
plane projection or examinations of
that being the cause of which simply
my own images recurr to puzzle me

obviously some things change
or maybe the song's sung over
different key or tune
mouths shaping the vowel notes

measure your worth as best you can
the last phrase takes you over the gap
a desert rises from between the lines
the empty quarter Dilmun reached into
before the axis shifted & the sand won out
back then perhaps yes that was the time
i know the saints were real & lived on earth
as I saw in a flash
the entire work as i have written it illuminated
given from the dream world half remembered

form then is what the present takes
seen as the past moment bursts forth
takes shape amid the air you freeze in
trapped by a history you cannot acknowledge
the poem become the life work
a hymn
                for you saint and
as i will always remember you
tragic in your age
you left your mark upon the world

where i saw it

i saw it saint and

your son saw it

mid-summer solstice over the heel stone
a whole epoch tied to the seasons
late september   dufferin county
fields bare from harvesting
dark furrows from the ploughing
andy & i sitting in the truck
counting up the orders for the city
cucumbers tomatoes carrots beets
no dance or festival to meet the season
only the OKTOBERFEST announced in Kitchener
instructions to jump on the tables & shout the songs out
how to get drunk
                the whole fucking nation that removed from
                                                /its roots

finally come to see
poets are such asocial beings
lost the gift of tongues the death of joy
no towns to wander thru & sing our songs to
somewhere perhaps that place or maybe
yes there are the fairs who listens
no place to sing the gift He gave me
blessed finally can i leave false death behind

trapped as we are in signs
our language multiplies above the cities
the letters meaningless words
we have less & less to say to one another

thus the buildings rise
distances between our separate dwellings reduced
made possible thru the death of speech
what was it someone said
if they're so civilized
why leave the lights on all night?
wander the streets lonely in our silence
fear of the unknown millions who surround you

saint rand you walked out too
as i do now walk
once as long ago your father saint reat did
lost his tongue that gift it had been given to him
down thru the darkness of these cities
we are sons so long our fathers dead
reach out thru a language left us homeless
to find it now again this age this time
speaking as we do a lost tongue
single voice of joy for the creation

❍ *birthday*

now that i have friends
that search ends
false veils of loneliness i wrapped myself in
orphaned thru denial of my mother
                                    my father

i age as the world turns
turning further from you saint rand
you have gone into a land i chose not to follow

this private hell or vision
ties you to a world that can't exist
so it is in these foreign times
we are strangers on the earth
turn from each other in our silence
hide behind our smiles our rage
i dreamt a cage formed round you
carried you down
into a nether world of cold fire
flames freezing your feet

you are the mirror of what you deny

trapped meat burning to be ether

all in a night i am taken
these voices scream in my ears
the choice of adjectives expletives
nothing is explicit
faces peer from darkness i would not remember

the choice made saint rand
we are together now
i relive each moment of that anguish

how friends asked me why? why always that one
that one her face does come again to haunt me
no it is another
forms overlap & blur

even as it is now distant i cannot touch it
there is a terror moves within me to take form
i fix it wrongly before its time

thus do we all saint rand
as you did place your terror outside you
deny ourselves we deny our gods
comes over me again
how i would age four kneel by my bed
pray no living creature would die
fear of my own rage & anger

father you are dead as i have killed you
you live again i recognize your face
peering out from photos i would bury
it is all so simple

only the man trapped in words recognizes that futility
as language was the prototype
perfect model of the robot run amuck
the tool that never could replace its master
become, as it were, a thing in itself
how i lay in anger, devastated
that night rob told me words need not exist
seen now as it is a substitution
we let it run our lives
                              wrongly

no there is no point finally
the systems that evolve made futile by that basic gap
never did learn how to touch beyond a one to one level
the social organism becomes a cancer
we attempt to simplify something that does not exist

age allows the grace of error
the chance we can correct what went before
your father died so lonely
he tried it got him nowhere
god how you hated him

we fail our fathers rand
lash out in our despair
destroy the very ones who might've helped us
as they would destroy us for reminding them who they are

what trapped bodies did you find there
flames to flow around you in your suffering
did you smile to see them

surely this was not the journey bunyan saw
denying as he did the joy of living
we take things to such extremes

yes i have enjoyed my suffering
it seems only fit
he who would achieve false sainthood to be denied it
by his own lack of vision

so it was the snake was misinterpreted
an early christian garbling of an older legend
how we must protect the sacred energy
energy seen now as something to be shunned

oh i do listen saint rand
but that vision
those bodies wrapped in chains
as language was the chain they did not see
how can they continue knowing as you must know
we must return again to human voice & listen
rip off the mask of words to free the sounds
we wear the chains as muscles rigidly

(i awoke with a strange dream. how we were all caught up in a time of
suffering we must pass thru to guard the sacred plants of regeneration.
it was morning. the light came thru the window where the cat lay
sleeping . . . .

as there is a dream i must awake from
question myself again (i always will)
so there is a door you knock upon saint rand
a tunnel you pass thru
catch a ride with poetry in the darkness
you ride the river okeanos
visit your father & the dark stranger
the cloaked one
he-who-rides-the-prow asleep
who is he that you do not know him
face averted

you found your father there
amid the birds the wailing
trailing the chain the sorrow round his breast
cried out to him then
passing as you were
poetry had shown you the way to go
a question only of returning
a pointless path to follow they said it leads but to death

such criticism illuminates nothing
being as it is at best a counterpoint
they create the legendary earth-two
you could step thru that warp in space & time
become one of them

yet you are here
beneath the land of men
reunited with your father again
as he with his & his with his
stretch backwards
to the beginning

"oh let me sing

oh let me dance

oh god please give me
a second chance

i was never for prayer
i was never for peace
i was never that happy
i was never that pleased

but oh let me sing

oh let me dance

oh god please give me
a second chance"

fasting sequence

1

left this morning for the spring
gather the water we need for survival
third day of an open-ended fast
such is the past we leave it behind us
walk among the aspens cedars
between the silver birches fill the buckets
carry them back to the car & home

last night we found auriga for the first time
the charioteer the chariot without a rider
or the young man goat on his right wrist
kids on his left
                    the one who stole the 7th sister away
capella its brightest star
now known to be a binary system
(possible origin of the missing pleiade
capella going nova around 2000 b.c.(?)
the temple of ptah oriented to its setting 5th millenium before christ
captured one of the seven sisters
sucked into his orbit
to spin around capella in a hundred days!)

we see him leaning against the fence
in his hand he holds the knife to slash the goat's throat
you are somewhere in the woods saint reat
finding the place the roads meet to carry on from

2

is there a confusion unstated or unseen
perseus perhaps & not auriga
holding the head of gorgon in the trees
these figures become apparent as glyphs
climbing down between the fissures
looking up to where the others stood
thot i saw a carving in the stone
same shape as cameloparadalis
unsure the moss so thick upon the rocks
my heart beat faster than i thot it could

i met you face to face among the trees
coming round the rock to find a way back up
you backed away
raised your fingers   a blessing or a curse
the worst moment of my life i stood there frightened

your face among the leaves your legs move slowly
see you smash the head beneath the stone
the up & down motion fascination
the writhing snakes & screams

helped you to a cup of water saint reat
you did not thank me
never thot you would

it is given freely

as it should be

3

two nights spent watching the constellations swing around polaris
"the shinie Casseiopea's chair'
                              "That starr'd Ethiop Queen that
                                                    / strove

to set her beauty's praise above
the Sea-nymphs;"
                        cepheus   auriga
draco the dragon
                        yu choo, the right hand pivot
lying near the constellation's centre
visible day & night
gazing up the central passage of cheops
the great pyramid, knum khufu
none of this made sense till i looked up
raised my head above the earth to study heaven

leaning on the orchard fence
smell of apples in the night air
dragon's tail wrapping round the lesser bear
included one time as the dragon's wings
you walk thru the trees behind me saint reat
over the fence into the field beyond

i thot you dead so long
your son saint rand living out his hell
i saw you in cepheus' out-stretched hands
seated in the inner throne of the five emperors
now you know it is not enough to die

our energy lives on
mingles with the stones & trees
we create mysteries each time we breathe
too much undone
you cannot rest
burn like the rest of us burn
turning round the pole star
"head foremost like a tumbler"

4

moving down to where the farmhouse stood
beside the ponds it lies in ruins
i sense your presence in the leaves saint reat
what someone told me
death is simply energy recycled   another state
realize that moment's joy it could be
fulfill my energy potential here on earth
ready to leave this plane behind

what were those last days like
we walk beside each other centuries
i see your history among the stars
it moves me to speak

everything bends toward this moment
surely as these words move worlds move
conjoin around a common point of reference which is praise
walk the earth as you did
sing your song
the book of days
the book of days
the book of days

5

find a focus then
my life runs not on circling
anchor feelings in my being
expell the poisons thru the fast
a change of diet change of plans
your outlook varies

locate polaris
& beyond that cepheus
one of its stars shaou wei (a minor guard)
the pole star of 19000 b.c.
when cepheus was called kapi, the ape-god, by the hindus
to reach that point again 4500 a.d.

concious of the stars we seek direction
walk among the woods beyond the valley
put up the apples into cider
what can we be but happy

this close to anger you recognize yourself for who you are
the thinner man confronts you in the mirror
saint reat i will know you when we meet again
as i must know myself when this life ends

so it is that you traverse a continent
gain understanding
                         travel to the bay of fundy
steve rafe paul & i
riding the train east
"isn't this where the sun comes from?"
i see your shadow fall from the west saint rand
just before you disappear
                              the riptide
are you carried under?

                         45 feet in 6 hours
watched the water pour out past the point
later drove down opposite cape split
the old shed where the ships were built
fran & tom & charles & barb &
the three of us (rafe already flying home)
this poem becomes a diary of a journey
personal it evolved impersonally
a longing as i will say must say please
saint rand stranded in that strange place
how would you call it
"a problem of resolution" ?
as tho the "i" the writer of these poems
controlled your destiny

i remember returning into sackville
fran hugged me
the lostness which had followed me everywhere
it was good to be there   a sense of contact
i felt grounded

                              but you saint rand
all night i tossed sleepless in my berth
aware the train carries me back home
concious as i was this morning
beginning this writing opposite quebec city
the troops   assassination
history changes nothing
i know only your story comes to me in sections
i have no control
                          so very aware of where you are
seeing your father's pain
knowing you blamed him wrongly
i watch the flat fields roll by the window
the white houses   the swings
the empty cans in the muddy ditch
near where we're stopping

mid-november the nights get colder
problems resolve themselves in terms of questions
you become rhetorical

driving back tonight over the hill
barely able to see thru the windshield of the car
the far wisps of light   are they constellations?

there is no consolation for you saint rand
tho i run in fear from this moment
i know the way out will be found
a question of letting energy mass
passing on & into   flow
learning living
i tried to free you prematurely
wrote the now discarded moment
posing falsely as a poem
knew then the terror of really living
how we substitute crisis for excitement
day to day

i remember the photo of my father
standing by the plunkett hotel
arms crossed   he is young & handsome
i have tried so hard to deny him

the bullshit   the lies
we feed ourselves on half-truths   illusions
never remember   was it the mahayana's said
true buddhahood lies in turning back
taking what you've found & turning it outward   into the world

it's really that simple
i suppose noone ever knew
that last door will open saint rand
if you really want it to

this morning talking with grant rob gestures at the snow
the world outside the window outside our heads
how we deny our energies denies we are part of it we are
grant weeping we are all close to fear
i fear not living more than living
fear that fear

all those people around you saint rand
watching the stranger walk out the door
so sure that they were dead they'd never tried the knob before
didn't believe it when you followed him thru
as noone ever believed you had come back again

the hate for your father gives way to longing
the longing makes you understand
he was a man who finally gave in
let despair overwhelm him
as it must if you live alone
don't let your love come home to you

praying i realize you are part of me
all of you as i'd foreseen
it is not the mystery that deepens
it is the sense of awe

sitting here in dufferin county

flows in from the cloudy sky

surrounds me

friends as footnotes

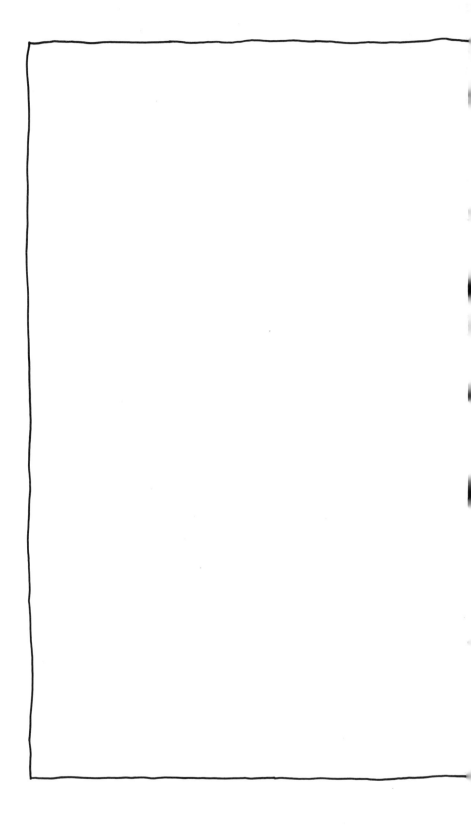

we buried terry beyond the orchard
mark & i digging in the half-frozen earth
laid her to rest as best we could
awkward phrases
                    it doesn't make much sense

fell asleep   late afternoon
came up for supper
first snow of the season falling
just beyond the edges of the room

the night before ellie's 29th birthday
death is such a sudden thing
lies seem useless   time-wasting
try to live your life honestly

saint and there is no point in hiding
the frozen faces   memories
the friends
there are so many things you don't understand
as if ignorance were mercy god rewarded with heaven
hell a function of wisdom
                    wisdom the quality of cursing

the white flows
over everything the color gathers
i had prayed it would
"first friend i've lost in years" visvaldis said
crying he held her body in his arms

there are no charms we know
no spells against the freak occurence
steps out of nowhere drags us down
we meet death
it is unexpected

you saints these poems are prayers
i don't give a fuck for your history

father in heaven
protect her soul
accept this gift of energy

three fingers

four bells

a spell against corruption

against hell

"in the midst of life we are in death"   draco
the dragon's wings clipped   the old lore's forgotten
craft as i told visvaldis that sense of pride gone
drove out the 401 the week before
west into darkness
rain all around us
ellie & i driving into what we did not know
trusting that white line to guide us

two days later ill in bed
something closes down around me
search the catalogue of "like"s
it is not there

always you are conscious the world is not encompassed
only the words you trust to take you thru
the next breath
                          moment
                                      time &
falling again saint and
your hand moves across my face
i am seized with trembling
death in the room
removes the window's glass

this is that place you'd dreaded
"something's" clear
that dark cloud which is nothing draws you nearer
as you knew it would

waiting for the phone to ring
you are ruled by your anticipation of what you'll miss
the futility of living one step out of sync with the present
your words rush ahead
prefacing your acts
prophesy your misdirection

stop

silence enters the room
fills up the corners you empty with noise &
rambling

gambling everything on listening

when the silence comes
it is silent

when death comes
there is absence

you can't hear

for saint reat & saint orm
this formless poem
death was
when it came near

for saint and
these twelve lines
for understanding

a thirteenth for luck

a fourteenth to fear

"older than adam's" older than me i am old
oh god today i am i am
the cold knowledge warms me
finite i reach for the infinite
wishing for your presence here beside me saint and
i am as old as you are old
the same hand moves inside our skins
each other's puppets we cling unknowingly
fill up our longing with whispering

a week's illness lingers
walking thru the street
the ghost presence beckons
where will you lead me

the one thing always i had feared
my own rashness
killing myself on whim
i carry shotgun shells in my pocket
blow my brains out in a department store
shocked faces my own surprise
folding slowly on the floor
silent as i had never been in life

i watch the streets fill with cars
the presence lingers
walks behind me home
who am alone when i choose to be
happy when i let joy in
knowing some change is imminent
fear that changing

later there is quietness & love
as later there should be
after the after
lord how i love thee lets love in

words archaic when the feeling is
we walk in shadows
or step out
                    free

today the words flow
links form no awareness of the letters
move as blocks   piling up
the poem compared to everything it isn't
being always what it is saint and
a conversation

                    is that love?

death is real or sensed is as death is always
a feeling's lived with
tingling in the cock
my pen scratches
writing

the taxi-driver in edmonton kept telling me about his baby
how she was expecting him to ball her
meanwhile he'd promised his wife a night out
after all it was her birthday

& last night
shaken by my reading in calgary
i dreamt you all dead
saint rand & saint and too
woke up not knowing what to do

there's nothing here

only the clouds stretch out towards the red horizon
sun already sunk from view
                                    the light blue turns darker
i can't see you
                    as the voices said   you left long ago
never did return
                    except to burn as thots i can't control
only to live inside my head

☁

insane line of pubic hair
my tongue goes down into language

speech that close to original birth
a sense of worth comes only with struggling

fuck you all saints
dream world of half remembered death
i loved you all
                    it nearly killed me

there is another world i've lived in all my life
took my own mind for my wife when just a kid
& hid there

made you up out of my breathing in that place
some sort of space made being bearable

the girl approached me when the reading ended
her own experience with christ
wanted to share it with me
loving as she said she did say
the religious sense in my poems
knowing you were all dead saint rand
what could i say

people how i lose myself in you
as stein saw it the difference between identity & entity
it is so much more soothing to live with memory

even now seated in this bus
having just flown into vancouver
the ache in my chest christ it always returns
like last night
barrie joy maureen & me getting drunk at mavis's place
there is a sense of space or time
goes missing

the i is always clear
it's just the we
forcing a retreat to memory
i define myself too often by what went before

she is right you know saint rand
stein did say
the hardest thing is making the present continuous
living day to day

now that you are dead
you are all here
no history to make it difficult

fences

cars

the window rattles in the pane

i want to explain
as composition does
only this present moment
actually past

i stop writing when i cease to flow

free to address you all by name
that day i want to

nd ryme

the final resolution

   way
         i suppose
f having it all make sense

enses

o surprises

he rhythm determined by
he last line

h i'm just fine i am i am
es & sure you know it'll be my pleasure

oh yes

uh
    no

i will look you up tho

looking out the window at the snow
late january   north vancouver
maybe a ship will come to harbor finally
make all our poems come true

sensing as i do the poem's levels
i am concious of the tone
dave pat & i talking
dave read me "letter to saint orm"
we'd talked for two days or
anyway it seemed you know
& pat had told me of the time in kaministiqua
her & dave living in a one room cabin
dave drove himself crazy writing 8 to 12 hours a day
she didn't know how to take him

memory is like this
trying to make it clear
barb married wayne a year before dave & denny met
& yet that party dave & denny threw
i did mention yes i did
barb came to   i'd come back to town   briefly
feeling in the room the tension barb & denny felt
what'd dave do?

& dave & denny
hell i never knew
visited them in montreal
their last try at making marriage work
just after, i guess, dave met pat
what does it matter?

it's only the moment we exist in
establishes flow
some form to make the words intelligible
remembering i began this section the day terry died
& here i am 3000 miles away still crying

you're dead

your life is lived

standing on the ferry's deck
carried me over to this island yesterday
what is it haunts me?
andy dave & i
our histories linked
will it always be this way
the two brothers & me friends
how many years   is it ten or twelve or
listen please saint and
i know you're dead but could i bother you one more time
one prayer for dave   one prayer for me
one prayer for pat   one prayer for andy
saint and
              could you set us free

early morning victoria's streets
we are all linked
all of us who use the language now   tied

talking with phyllis   the kropotkin poems
how she'd first realized the importance of questions reading joyce's
                                                    "portrait"

focus in   language "is" not "was"
words that particular form the sky is
grey & restless

the speech is gathering
what'll we say next time
after the city's dead
after the fantasy that is north america crumbles
what'll we do if we're left
knowing the people we thot weren't listening weren't

it is simple
hell a complex vision of heaven
operating as a curse does
                              brings you down

we spend too much time comforting each other
thinking that way i did riding the bus out this evening
people none of whom i knew
we sat beside each other
wrapped in our separate silences

"people people where do you go
 before you believe in what you know"

all this talking in my head   how much of it said when i die
some lonely night like this
                              waves wash the deck
listing

sleepless night nothing takes shape
the poem is spoken as an ode is
to love

          o god the trees the gentle birches oaks the
language lung wage everything i owe to you o
everyone   every one of you
the night takes form in poems is sung is
as the heart is
beating leaving you
a song

sung as the sullen art gains presence
knowing you alive my life my saints my
witnessed all your deaths each night for weeks
the agony
          living now as energy
flows from my fingers into these poems

oh god you are dead you are dead dead dead
christ you are dead you are dead dead dead
what can i do who shall i be i can't see you any more
no direction sign or longing
only the space behind my eyes screaming
you are dead you are dead you are dead dead dead
no joy to feel tho i free you gladly
no chain of words to bind you to me
how can i live who cannot be without you
knowing you are dead you are dead you are dead dead dead
dead you are dead
no longer to live or walk in comfort
only the skies empty my tears
hell i could fill the space with moaning
oh you are gone & i am left
lonely father
i am lonely father
father i am lonely
knowing they are dead
they are dead dead dead
they are dead
they are dead
they are dead dead dead
& i'm lonely father
i am lonely father
father i am lonely
lonely father
i am

as there are words i haven't written
things i haven't seen
so this poem continues
a kind of despair takes over
the poem is written in spite of

all the words i once believed were saints
language the holy place of consecration
gradually took flesh
becoming real

scraptures behind me
i am written free
so many people saying to me they do not understand
the poem they can't get into
i misplace it three times

this is not a spell
it is an act of desperation
the poem dictated to me by another will
a kind of being writing is
opposite myself i recognize these hands
smash the keys in
the necessary assertion of reality

ah reason there is only feeling
knowing the words are
                              i am
this moment is
everything present & tense
i write despite my own misgivings
say things as they do occur
the mind moves truly
is it free

nothing's free of presence
others pressing in
your friends assert themselves as loving you are tortured with
gradually you learn to enjoy

thus you write a history
use words you've used before
your own voice speaking in the morning whispering
holy god i do love you then praise you
take up this gift of joy
not to judge or be judged by
you who have given me lips   a tongue
the song sings because of you
all theory denies you
that struggle's truly won
once what's begun is done

CANADIAN CATALOGUING IN PUBLICATION DATA

Nichol, B.P., 1944-1988
 The martyrology books 1 & 2

Second ed.
Poems.
ISBN 1-55245-028-7

I. Title.

PS8527.I32M3 1998   C811'.54   C98-930570-8
PR9199.3.N52M3 1998

To order or read online versions of Coach House Books,
please visit http://www.chbooks.com
For more traditional interaction, contact
Coach House Books
401 Huron St. on bpNichol Lane, Toronto, Ont M5S 2G5
Telephone: 1 800 367 6360

Jerry Ofo designed & illustrated the text of this book.
Gordon Robertson designed the cover.
The author has deleted certain sections of books I & II and
rewritten others as well as correcting some typographical
errors that appeared in the first edition for this second
edition of 1977 which was published with the assistance of
The Canada Council and the Ontario Arts Council.
First printed in the spring of 1972 in an edition of 1000
copies.